PAIRED PASSAGES

Grade 1

Credits
Content Editor: Jeanette Moore Ritch, M.S. Ed.
Copy Editor: Paulette McGee, Julie B. Killian

Visit *carsondellosa.com* for correlations to Common Core, state, national, and Canadian provincial standards.

Carson-Dellosa Publishing LLC
PO Box 35665
Greensboro, NC 27425 USA
carsondellosa.com

ISBN 978-1-4838-3065-0
03-317171151

Table of Contents

Introduction

As students sharpen their reading comprehension skills, they become better readers. Improving these skills has never been more important as teachers struggle to meet the rigorous college- and career-ready expectations of today's educational standards.

This book offers pairings of high-interest fiction and nonfiction passages that will appeal to even the most reluctant readers. The passages have grade-level readability. Follow-up pages promote specific questioning based on evidence from the passages.

Throughout the book, students are encouraged to practice close reading, focusing on details to make inferences from each passage separately and then as a set. The text-dependent questions and activities that follow the passages encourage students to synthesize the information they have read, leading to deeper comprehension.

How to Use This Book

Three types of pairings divide this book: fiction with nonfiction, nonfiction with nonfiction, and fiction with fiction. The book is broken down further into 22 sets of paired passages that are combined with follow-up questions and activities. Each reading passage is labeled *Fiction* or *Nonfiction*.

The passages in this book may be used in any order but should be completed as four-page sets so that students read the passages in the correct pairs. The pairs of passages have been carefully chosen and each pair has topics or elements in common.

Two pages of questions and activities follow each pair of passages to support student comprehension. The questions and activities are based on evidence that students can find in the texts. No further research is required. Students will answer a set of questions that enable comprehension of each of the two passages. The questions range in format and include true/false, multiple choice, and short answer. The final questions or activities ask students to compare and contrast details or elements from the two passages.

Assessment Rubric

Use this rubric as a guide for assessing students' work. It can also be offered to students to help them check their work or as a tool to show your scoring.

4	_____ Independently reads and comprehends grade-level texts _____ Easily compares and contrasts authors' purposes _____ Uses higher-order thinking skills to link common themes or ideas _____ References both passages when comparing and contrasting _____ Skillfully summarizes reading based on textual evidence
3	_____ Needs little support for comprehension of grade-level texts _____ Notes some comparisons of authors' purposes _____ Infers broad common themes or ideas _____ Connects key ideas and general themes of both passages _____ Uses textual evidence to summarize reading with some support
2	_____ Needs some support for comprehension of grade-level texts _____ Understands overt similarities/differences in authors' purposes _____ Links stated or obvious common themes or ideas _____ Compares and contrasts both passages with support _____ Summarizes reading based on textual evidence with difficulty
1	_____ Reads and comprehends grade-level text with assistance _____ Cannot compare or contrast authors' purposes _____ Has difficulty linking common themes or ideas _____ Cannot connect the information from both passages _____ Is unable to use textual evidence to summarize reading

Birds of a Feather

Some friends are the same, and some friends are different. Joe and Lu are little birds. They both hatched from their eggs just five weeks ago. They came from nests in the same yard, but they grew up in different trees.

Joe and Lu look very different, but they are good friends. Joe has deep blue feathers. Lu has bright red feathers. Joe is a blue jay. Lu is a cardinal. Joe likes to eat acorns. His beak is made for opening them. Lu likes to eat fruit. His beak is a little smaller than Joe's beak.

They both love to eat one kind of bird food. They love to eat seeds! Joe and Lu meet at the same bird feeder every day. This is when they have a little fun. They fly from the tree to the flower bush. Then, they fly back to the bird feeder to eat with their beaks!

The birdbath is where birds play in the water. Many birds get a drink of water there too. Joe and Lu go to the birdbath often. On sunny days, they splash in the birdbath!

Eat with a Beak

Bird beaks are not all the same shape. Beaks are useful tools. Birds use them for many purposes. Birds use their beaks to make nests. They use their beaks to fix their feathers. They use their beaks to gather food.

Birds eat many different kinds of food. Their beaks give us clues. A beak can be a hammer. A beak can be a hook. A beak can even be a spear.

Look at a bird's **bill**, or beak. The beak shape helps us understand what a bird eats and what kind of bird it is. Here are three common beak shapes:

Probe

Hummingbirds have long beaks. Their beaks look like straws. The hummingbirds sip nectar from flowers.

Chisel

Woodpeckers have very strong beaks. Their beaks look like chisels. The woodpeckers make holes in trees to get insects.

Spear

Herons have very long bills. Their bills have hooked points at the end. The herons can snag fish.

Name _____

Circle the correct answer.

1. Birds use their beaks to

   A. hide from cats.

   B. point to trees.

   C. eat food.

2. Birds can splash in a

   A. birdbath.

   B. bird feeder.

   C. birdhouse.

Use the word bank to complete the sentences.

acorns	bill	fruit

3. Another word for a **beak** is a _____.

4. Joe likes to eat _____ and seeds.

5. Lu likes to eat _____ and seeds.

6. Write a sentence about how Joe and Lu are alike.

   _____

   _____

   _____

Name _____

7. Look at each bird. Write or draw about the food it likes to eat. Then, draw what each bird's beak looks like.

Bird	It eats	Its beak looks like
 woodpecker		
 heron		
 hummingbird		
 blue jay		

8. Are the two passages alike? How do you know?

_____

_____

_____

_____

A Garden for Grace

Grace learned about plants on a field trip. Her school went to a botanical garden. Grace saw the flowers. They had bright colors. The flowers were from all over the world!

Grace liked the trees. She even saw a giant kapok tree! She had heard about this tree before. Her teacher read a picture book to her class. The tree was very tall. It grew in Brazil in the Amazon rain forest.

Grace planted a few seeds in her yard. She got the seeds from the store by her house. She really wanted to grow that giant kapok tree! Instead, she planted flowers. The seed bag said "Mixed Flowers." She did not know what each flower would look like. She watered her new garden every day.

Then, the seeds popped out of the dirt. One type of seed was growing fast. The flower grew each day. Soon, it was taller than Grace! Then, it bloomed. It was yellow. It was not as **huge** as a kapok tree, but it was very big. It was 6 feet (1.8 m) tall. The yellow flower glowed over her head. It was a pretty **sunflower**!

The Kapok Tree

The Amazon rain forest is in South America. Much of the rain forest is in Brazil. The rain forest is home to many plants. Flowers and trees grow there.

One tree that lives in the rain forest can grow 13 feet (4 m) each year. It can grow to 200 feet (61 m) tall. It is called a **kapok** tree. This giant tree is in Mexico and Africa too.

The tree is large. The bottom of the tree is wide. In fact, it is 9 or 10 feet (2.7 or 3 m) wide. Many animals live in the tree. Some frogs like the tree. Birds fly around the tree.

Some bats like it too. The bats like the smell of the tree. It is stinky! The smell comes from the flowers. The tree buds have white and pink flowers. The tree also has fruit. Each piece of fruit can have 200 seeds!

Name _____

Circle the correct answer.

1. The Amazon rain forest is in

    A. South America.

    B. Mexico.

    C. Africa.

2. A kapok tree can grow

    A. 10 feet tall.

    B. 200 feet tall.

    C. 9 feet tall.

Use the word bank to complete the sentences.

huge	kapok	sunflower

3. Another word for **big** is _____.

4. A _____ is tall and yellow.

5. The _____ is a kind of tree.

6. Write a sentence about a sunflower and a kapok tree.

_____

_____

_____

7. Look back at both passages. Complete the graphic organizer.

	Sunflower	Kapok Tree
What color is the plant?		
How tall is it?		
Where does it grow?		
Draw a picture.		

8. How are the sunflower and the kapok tree different?

_____

_____

_____

_____

Fishing in the River

The river water was still. The rain stopped. It was cloudy and dim. The sun was going up into the sky. It was early in the morning. Murphy **cast**, or threw, his line into the water. He was with his dad. They liked to fish in the morning the best. Murphy had not caught a fish yet.

His dad showed him how to put a new worm on the line. His dad also drove the boat in the river. He had a special card called a **license**. This card was important because it allowed him to drive. The boat had a motor. It made a *vroom* sound in the water!

Now, the boat was in a new spot. Murphy cast his line back into the water. His dad cast a line into the water too. *Chomp!* A fish bit Murphy's hook! Murphy pulled the fishing pole back. He brought up the line. A fish was on the end of the line! It was a big bass. His dad was very proud of him.

How to Fish

Fishing is a sport that many people like to do. Some people fish for fun. Other people fish to get food. People fish in rivers, oceans, and lakes. Some people fish on boats. Others fish from docks. If you want to fish, you have to do a few things.

First, you need a fishing pole. You can make one with string and a stick. You can buy one from a store. A hook goes on the end of the line.

Next, you will need **bait**. Bait is food for the fish. People use corn, worms, and other bait for the hook.

Then, you can **cast**. Casting is when the person fishing throws the **line**, or string, into the water. Toss the line gently into the water by flicking the fishing pole with your hand and arm.

Finally, you will have a fish biting on your line. You will have to reel, or pull, the fish in by turning the knob on your fishing pole. Or, you can pull in the string. It is exciting to go fishing!

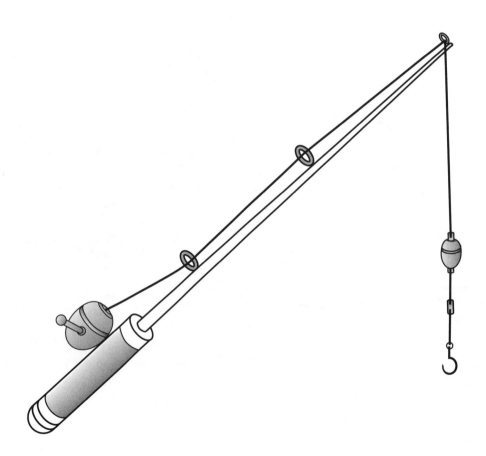

Name _____

Circle the correct answer.

I. A fishing **line** is

    A. wide.

    B. string.

    C. reel.

2. When you cast a line, you

    A. see the line.

    B. hold the line.

    C. toss the line.

Use the word bank to complete the sentences.

bait	cast	license

3. A worm is a kind of _____.

4. Murphy _____ his fishing line into the water.

5. A _____ is an important card for driving.

6. Write a sentence about being on a boat.

_____

_____

_____

7. Imagine you are going on a fishing trip. What will you need to bring with you? Use the information from both passages to make a list.

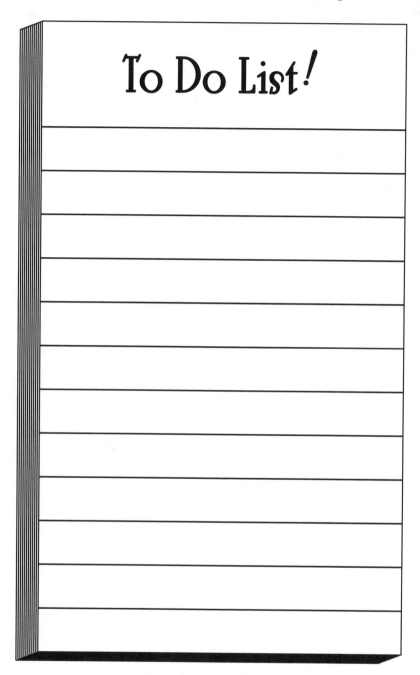

To Do List!

8. How are the two passages different?

_____

_____

_____

Uncle Matt

Matt is Mom's cousin. But, my brother and I always call him Uncle Matt. I think it is because he is older than the other cousins. He laughs and plays with us. He is fun to be around.

Uncle Matt has a special talent. He can play the piano very well. He learned to play the piano when he was four years old. He had a piano teacher. Her name was Mrs. Green.

Mrs. Green taught him to play many songs. Uncle Matt played songs in front of big groups of people. He **performed**. He liked to be onstage.

He is older now, and he plays songs for us. He uses the piano at Grandma's house. The piano is in the living room. Uncle Matt sits on the long piano bench. He plays songs for us to dance to.

Sometimes, we sing with him. He thinks that I really like the piano, and I should learn how to play. He is going to teach me!

Music Lessons

Kids can learn to play songs. They can learn to play instruments. Learning to play helps kids get skills for making music. Kids learn the words to songs. They can also play music notes.

But, kids learn more than this. Music makes the brain stronger. Kids can take music lessons. Even babies can take music lessons!

Kids can take lessons on all kinds of instruments. Kids can play the drums and learn to play to the beat. Kids can play the guitar and learn new songs. Kids can even play the trumpet or the violin! The piano is also a good instrument for taking lessons.

Music lessons help kids practice skills. Kids practice with teachers. Some kids practice with computers. Some kids take lessons with other kids.

Music practice makes kids play better. Some kids want to write their own songs. Music is fun for all!

Circle the correct answer.

I. Uncle Matt is

    A. Mom's cousin.

    B. Mom's brother.

    C. Mom's friend.

2. Kids can practice music and take lessons with

    A. computers or games.

    B. teachers or games.

    C. teachers or computers.

Use the word bank to complete the sentences.

house	performed	practice

3. Music lessons are great for _____.

4. Uncle Matt uses the piano at Grandma's _____.

5. Kids have _____ music onstage.

6. Write a sentence about a musical instrument you have heard or played.

_____

_____

_____

7. Look back at both passages. Make a list of some of the benefits of taking music lessons and playing music.

8. Based on the two passages, what did you learn about music?

_____

_____

_____

Miguel's Haircut

Miguel was getting ready for first grade. His hair was long in the summer. The hair stuck up on the top of his head! Miguel tucked his hair behind his ears. His hair was short in June. By September, it was too long. Aunt Rosa said he needed a haircut right away. He could not start school looking like this!

First, Rosa called the barber. A **barber** is a person who cuts hair. The barber said to come in on Saturday at 2:00 pm. This was perfect. School started on Monday.

Then, Miguel went to the barbershop. He sat in a tall chair. The barber put a cloth around Miguel's neck. It covered the front of his chest.

After Miguel sat in the chair, the barber started to **trim**, or cut, Miguel's hair with small scissors. The scissors were sharp! Miguel had to sit still. The hair fell onto the cloth and the floor.

When the barber was finished, Miguel looked in the mirror. He looked like a new boy! He was ready for school now.

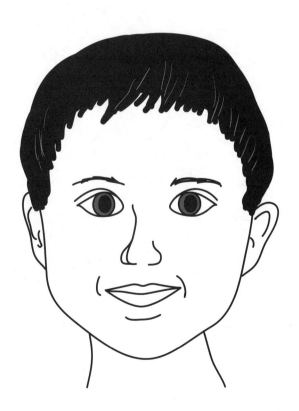

Barbers and Hairdressers

Barbers are people who cut hair. Hairdressers cut hair too. It is their job to cut hair. Hairdressers also style hair and make it look nice. They can even add **dye** to hair. Dye makes hair a new color!

Barbers can go to school to learn to cut hair. Hairdressers can do this too. Some schools have salons in them. The salon is where barbers and hairdressers practice. They can practice cutting hair on people. They can practice cutting hair on dolls. The teachers show the students how to cut hair the right way.

It is important for people to shampoo hair. Hairdressers and barbers wash their hair. Sometimes, they use spray or gel. They have many brushes. They also use the hair dryer. It dries hair quickly.

Hairdressers and barbers talk to people. They work with people all day. They are friendly. They smile. And, they want to make hair look wonderful!

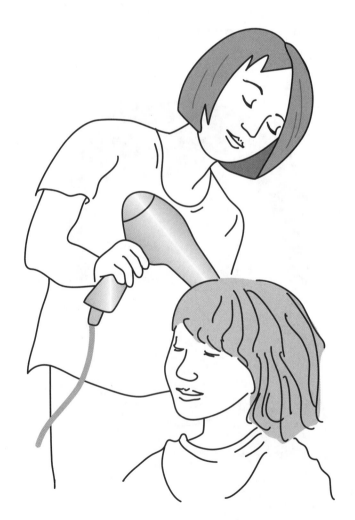

Name _____

Circle the correct answer.

1. Miguel got a haircut in

    A. April.

    B. June.

    C. September.

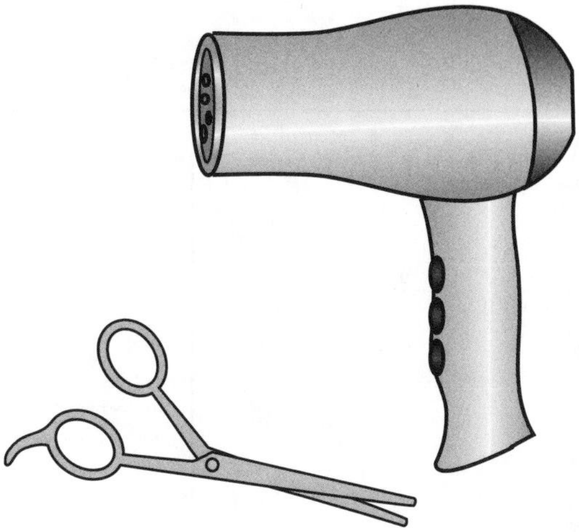

2. Miguel went to a

    A. hairdresser.

    B. barbershop.

    C. hair washer.

Use the word bank to complete the sentences.

barber	dye	trim

3. Miguel's hair was long, and it needed a _____.

4. A _____ cuts hair.

5. A hairdresser can add _____ to change hair color.

6. Write a sentence about what a barber or a hairdresser does.

_____

_____

_____

7. Draw pictures of three of the barber's tools you learned about in the two passages.

8. Based on the two passages, what may the barber have done to cut Miguel's hair?

_____

_____

_____

9. How are the two passages alike?

_____

_____

_____

Jamaica's Birthday

Jamaica has a party planned for Saturday. Saturday is her birthday! Ten friends, or **guests**, will come to her house. They will play games. Jamaica wants to play hide-and-seek. She wants to play with toys too. The kids will go on her playset in the backyard.

Then, they will eat food. Jamaica's mom will make macaroni and cheese. She also plans to make a fruit salad. The kids will have full bellies! But, they need room for dessert.

After the friends eat food, they will eat cake. Jamaica's mom enjoys baking cakes. The cake is going to be chocolate. Frosting will be on top of the cake. It will be delicious!

The 10 friends may bring gifts for Jamaica. Jamaica looks forward to opening the gifts. She will open the birthday cards first. Then, she will open the gifts. Mom will help gather the scraps of **gift wrap**, or pretty paper. Jamaica cannot wait for Saturday!

Having a Party

Parties are great fun! If you are going to have one, make sure that you are ready. Much has to be done to prepare.

First, make a list of friends. Then, write a card for each one. The card is called an **invitation**. It has the time and date of the party. The card will also show where the party will be. Some people put their phone numbers on the cards. Friends can call and say if they can come.

Next, you need to make another list. This list has all of the things you need for the party. You can make a list of food such as pizza, salad, and juice. You can make a list of party items such as plates, napkins, and spoons.

You also have to decorate, or hang art and ribbon. Balloons are good to use. Some kids have little toys and noisemakers. Other kids draw pictures and make crafts. All of these things make for a fun party!

Name _____

Circle the correct answer.

1. Birthday party food can be

    A. wedding cake.

    B. birthday cupcakes.

    C. candles.

2. Jamaica's mom enjoys baking

    A. cookies.

    B. cakes.

    C. buns.

Use the word bank to complete the sentences.

gift wrap	guests	invitation

3. The friends are _____ at the party.

4. Mom will gather the _____ after the presents have been opened.

5. Each guest gets a card, or _____.

6. Write a sentence about what is written on an invitation.

_____

_____

Name _____

7. Imagine you are planning a party for your best friend. Use the information from both passages to make a list.

List of Things to Do

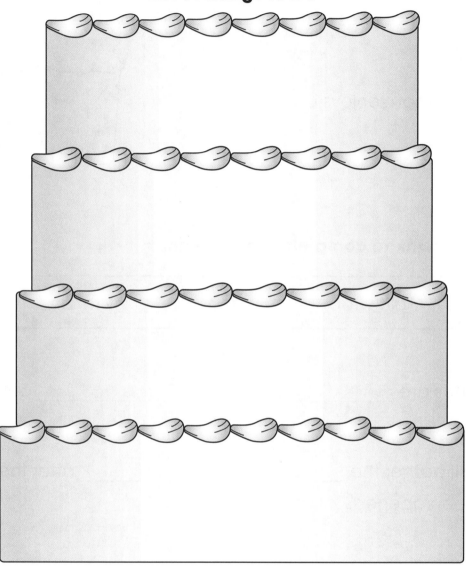

8. How do the two passages remind you of a party you have gone to? Use information from both passages in your answer.

_____

_____

_____

Roadwork

Jon picked up his backpack. It was hanging next to his jacket in the hallway. He put on his jacket, zipped it up, and got ready for school.

"Jon, it's time to get in the car!" Dad called.

"I am almost ready, Dad!" Jon replied.

Jon put on his shoes and tied the laces. He opened the front door.

"Here I come!" Jon waved across the lawn.

Soon, he was in the car with his dad. They put on their seatbelts. Dad drove down the road toward the school.

"Look in the road, Dad!" Jon said. A big yellow sign said "Construction Work Ahead." Construction is roadwork. The men and women construction workers were fixing the road. Dad slowed down the car.

"It looks like roadwork. We will have to take a detour," Dad said.

"What is a detour?" Jon asked.

"A **detour** is a different way to get to a place," Dad explained.

Dad drove to the side of the road. He followed the signs along the roads. He drove the car on the new **route**, or way, to school. It took a little longer, but Jon still made it to school on time.

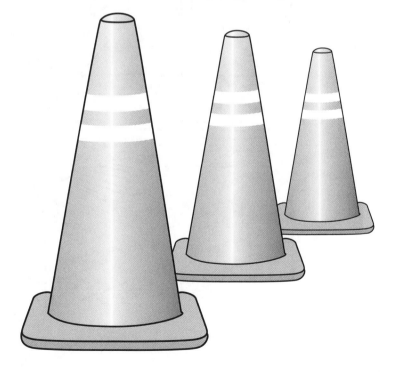

Construction Zone

Construction zones are places where roadwork is happening. Roadwork happens for many reasons. The workers fix holes in the streets. The workers fix the curbs. Sometimes, sewers or pipes need to be **repaired**, or fixed. The pipes are under the roads.

Crews use many kinds of trucks. The trucks are good for roadwork. Dump trucks carry dirt and rocks in the back. They can also carry pebbles and sand.

A loader is a big machine. Loaders have buckets and scoop dirt. Bulldozers are big machines too. They can rip up the dirt and roads. All of the trucks are big!

Any of these trucks can be in construction zones. A lot of dirt can be there too. Sometimes, rocks are in the dirt.

Workers can be in the roads and on the sidewalks. The roadwork is needed so that cars can pass safely on the roads. Construction on roads slows down cars. But, it is important to keep the roads safe.

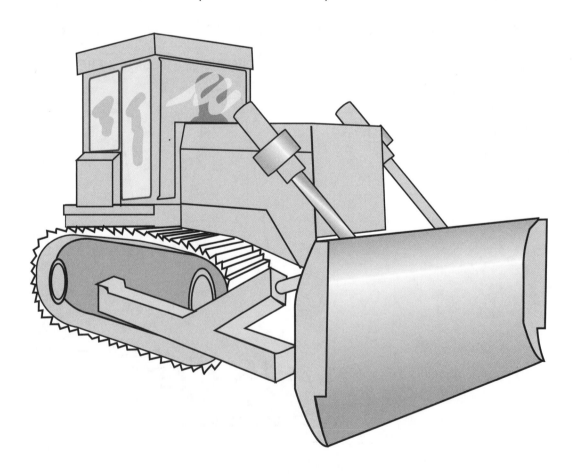

Name _____

Circle the correct answer.

1. Loaders

    A. have buckets that can scoop up dirt.

    B. can rip up dirt and roads.

    C. can fix curbs.

2. A dump truck can be filled with

    A. cars.

    B. road signs.

    C. dirt and rocks.

Use the word bank to complete the sentences.

> detour   repair   route

3. They rode their bikes along the bike _____.

4. Construction workers _____ holes in the road.

5. Jon's dad had to take a _____ to get to school.

6. Write a sentence about what roadwork looks like.

_____

_____

_____

7. Imagine that you are riding on a bus. You look out the window. You see roadwork. Write or draw what you may see based on the two passages you read.

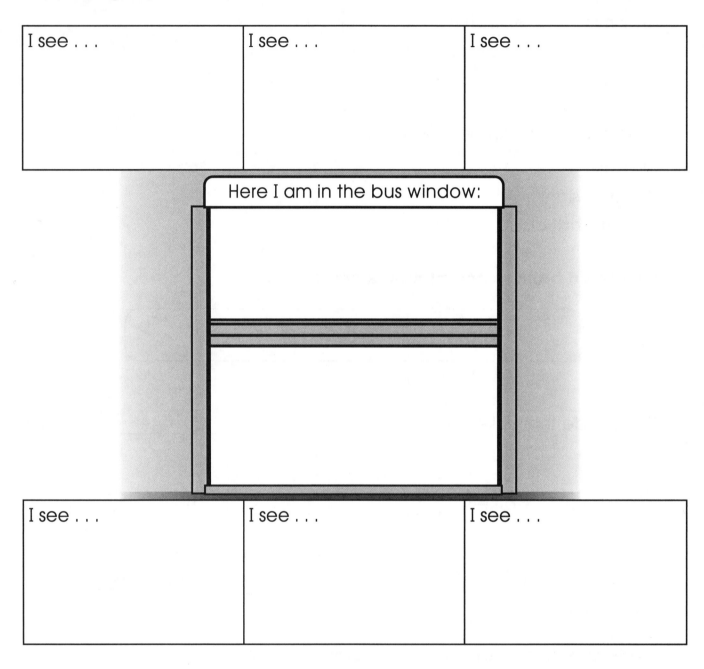

I see . . .	I see . . .	I see . . .

Here I am in the bus window:

I see . . .	I see . . .	I see . . .

8. What did you learn about construction work from the two passages?

_____

_____

_____

Ant Facts

Ants are in our yards. Ants are outside at school. Sometimes, ants come into our homes. They often show up at picnics. Ants are everywhere!

Ants are in the same family as bugs you would never guess—bees! They are also in the wasp family. They do not fly, but members of their bug family do.

Ants look for **crumbs**, or small pieces of food. They also eat fruit and seeds. They even eat other bugs. Yuck! Ants tell each other where the food is. They **collect**, or gather, the food. That is their job. They bring the food back to the queen ant. She is in charge of the ant home. She is a large ant.

There are more than 10,000 kinds of ants. Carpenter ants make nests in wood. They can build nests in buildings. Army ants do not have homes. They just march and find food. Yellow crazy ants make super houses. Some people would say that is crazy!

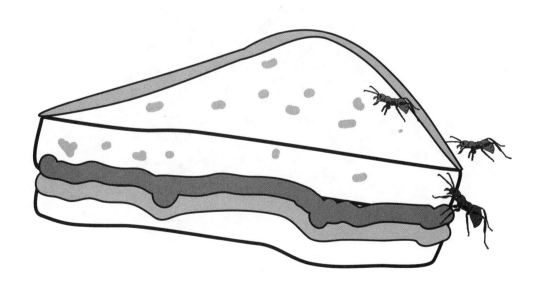

Ant Workers

Ants look like little black bugs. But, they are more than just bugs. Ants are hard workers. They are strong. They can carry about 20 times their own weight! They live together in groups. Each ant has a job to do.

Ants are able to **communicate**, or talk, to each other. They give off pheromones, or smells, to communicate. Ants can tell each other about where to find food. They can tell each other about danger ahead.

A queen ant lives in each ant home. She is a large ant! She makes baby ants by laying eggs. The queen ant can make thousands of baby ants!

Ants eat leaves. They eat dead bugs. They eat fruit and small crumbs of food. Sometimes, ants can make it into kitchens. They can get into cafeterias. They can get into cars. They look for little bits of food. So, be sure to watch your plate if you are at a picnic! Ants are always hungry.

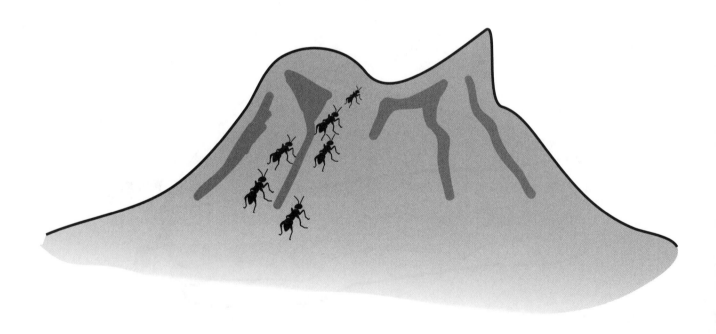

Name _____

Circle the correct answer.

I. Ants gather

    A. grass.

    B. food.

    C. dirt.

2. Carpenter ants make nests in

    A. anthills.

    B. wood.

    C. grass.

Use the word bank to complete the sentences.

> collect   communicate   crumb

3. Ants _____ a lot of food to bring to the anthill.

4. A _____ is a small piece of food.

5. Ants are able to _____ with each other.

6. Write a sentence about what you think the grass looks like from an ant's eyes.

_____

_____

7. Look back at the two passages. Draw the types of food an ant can eat. Write the name of each food.

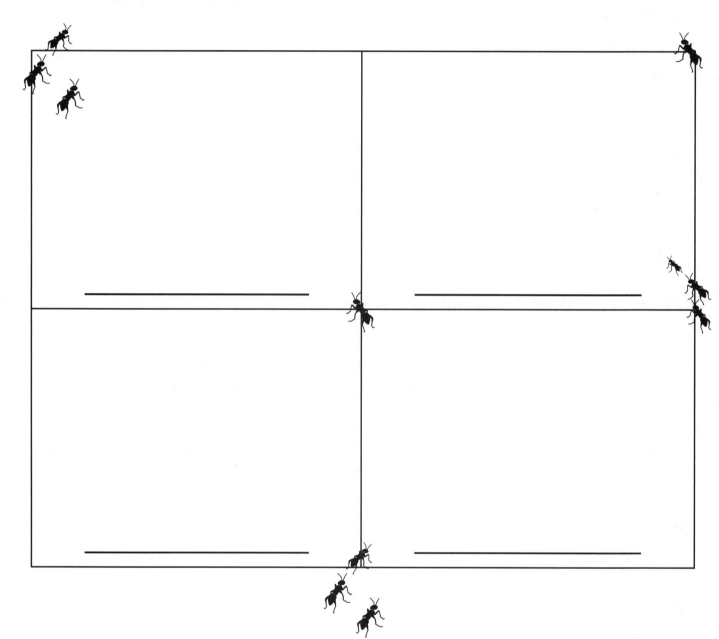

8. How are the two passages alike?

_____

_____

_____

Moving Day

Moving to a new place can be very exciting. But, moving is a lot of work! Moving day is a big day. It is a time to move a lot of things. People move books. They move toys. They move beds. They move much more!

When people move, they have a new place to live. Someone different has their old homes. People who move put their belongings in their new home. Moving day is busy for everyone!

People can move to a house down the road. People can move to a town nearby. They can even move to another state or country!

People may stack boxes in their driveway. They may put boxes on the sidewalks too. The **movers**, or people who move things, put the boxes into moving trucks. Sometimes, movers need to fill more than one truck. Movers bring everything to the new home on moving day.

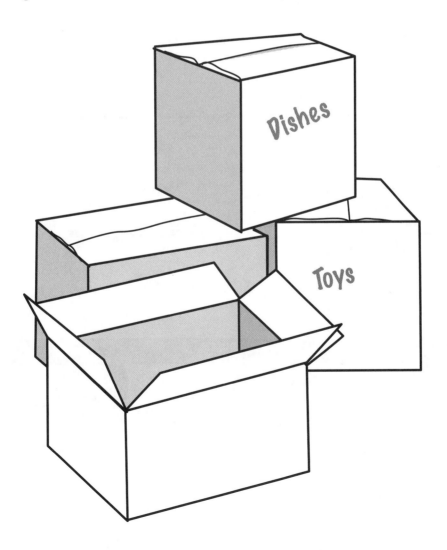

The Moving Truck

Moving trucks come in handy. People are ready to move from one house to another. People can **rent**, or borrow, moving trucks. Moving trucks are big. Some are 26 feet (7.9 m) long! A moving truck is shaped like a big box. People can put a lot of things inside a moving truck.

A moving truck is made of metal. Movers put boxes in the truck. They stack the boxes in nicely. Some people use big bins to pack their things. Bins can be made out of plastic.

Many times, a driver needs a special **license**, or card, to drive a truck. If the truck is very big, then it is important for the mover to have the truck license.

People fill moving trucks with many things. They put in chairs. They put in tables. They put in toys. They put in clothes. People can move everything!

Circle the correct answer.

1. Sometimes, movers need more than one truck to

    A. buy.

    B. fill.

    C. wash.

2. Movers _____ boxes in the truck.

    A. stack

    B. crush

    C. throw

Use the word bank to complete the sentences.

license	movers	rent

3. The driver has a special truck _____.

4. People borrow or _____ trucks when they need to move.

5. The _____ bring the boxes into the new house.

6. Write a sentence about a time you moved or what you think it would feel like to move someplace new.

_____

_____

7. Draw or write items from the two passages that can be placed in a moving truck.

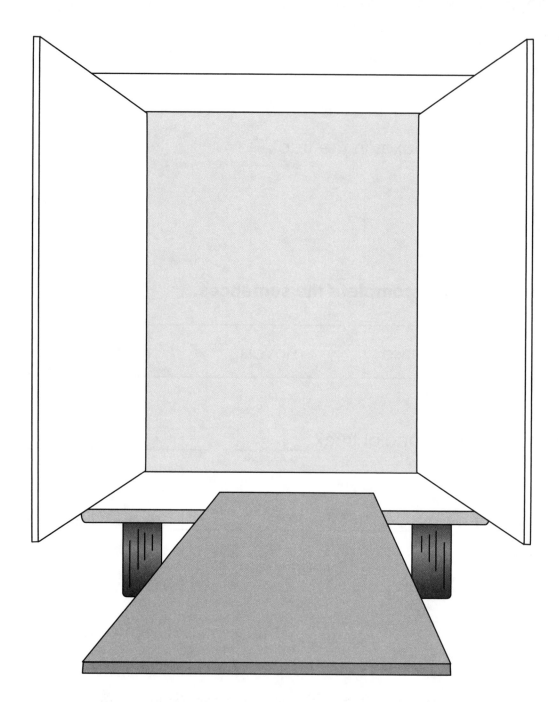

8. What did you learn about moving from the two passages?

_____

_____

_____

At the Museum

A museum is a place where people can visit. It is a place where kids can explore and learn new things. A museum has many things to look at such as artwork. It may also have sculptures.

Sometimes, a museum has gardens and places to sit. Some bigger museums have gift shops. Sometimes, they have places to eat in a museum. The food can be pretty like the art.

Some art museums have paintings. The paintings are made with different kinds of paint. Oil paintings are made with oil paint. The colors are thick on the paper. Watercolor paintings have watery color. The colors are light on the paper.

A discovery museum is another type of museum. It may have games for students. It may have science labs and shows. It may even have dinosaur bones!

A museum has a lot to see. A museum is a fun place to visit.

The Museum of Modern Art

The Museum of Modern Art is also called the MOMA. It is in New York City. Many **famous**, or well-known, kinds of art are in the MOMA. A special painting by a man named Vincent Van Gogh is there. He made a painting called *Starry Night*. The painting has a lot of blue colors and yellow too. It shows the night sky.

The MOMA has an **art lab**, or a place to make art. Kids can go to the art lab to play with art tools. They can explore any art **medium**, or kinds of paints and crayons. The lab is for playing with new kinds of art tools. The MOMA offers classes for kids and parents.

Kids have the chance to use a lot of paint and crayons. They can make art and look at art. So many rooms are filled with art! The colors and sizes make all of the art interesting and different. This is a very special museum.

Name _____

Circle the correct answer.

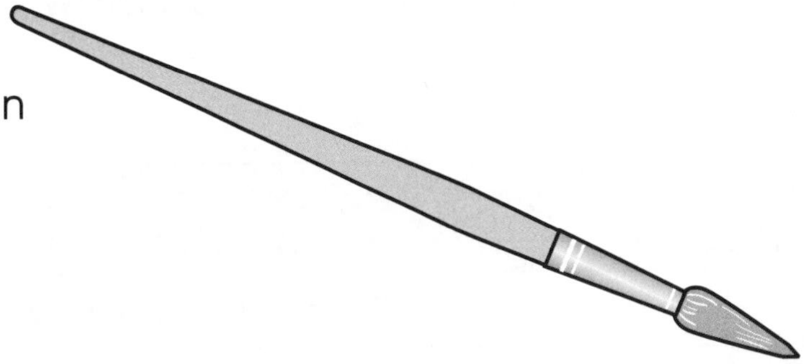

1. The Museum of Modern Art is in

   A. a garden.

   B. the country.

   C. New York City.

2. Oil paintings are made with

   A. thick oily paints.

   B. light watery paints.

   C. crayons.

Use the word bank to complete the sentences.

art lab	famous	medium

3. You can paint with any art medium in the _____.

4. Van Gogh has a _____ painting called *Starry Night*.

5. Kids can use crayons as a _____ for their artwork.

6. Write a sentence about what you might see in a museum.

   _____

   _____

   _____

Name _____

7. Look back at both passages. Draw four things you might see in a museum.

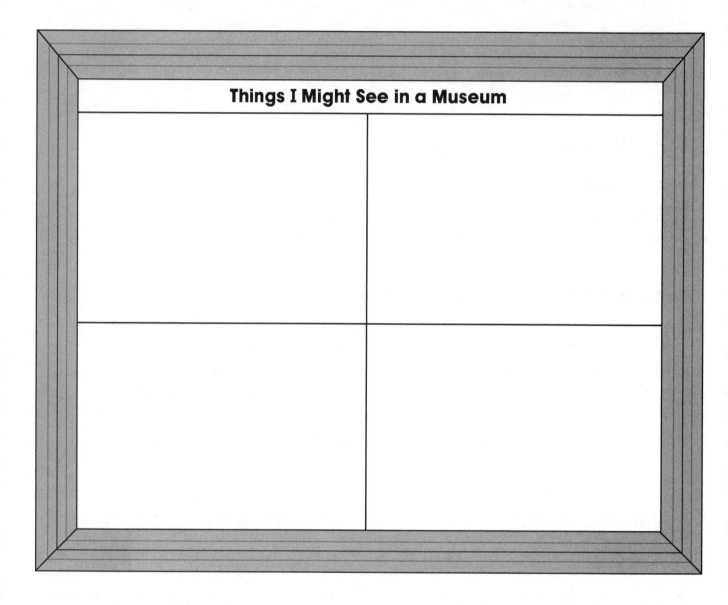

Things I Might See in a Museum

8. How are the two passages different? How are they alike?

_____

_____

_____

Baseball Gear

A lot of people love to play baseball. Some people like to watch games. The baseball players wear gear. They have many kinds of gear.

Cleats, or baseball sneakers, are great for players when they run. The bottoms of the shoes have spikes. The players can also wear helmets. A helmet is helpful for when players are hitting the ball with the bat. The helmet is important. The ball is very hard and is made of yarn and cork. A baseball weighs about 5 ounces (141.7 g). Players wear jerseys. Jerseys are shirts. They are made of cotton and other materials. They have the team name on them.

Players like to use bats. Some bats are made from ash wood. Players also use baseball gloves. They are leather. They have small pockets where the ball fits. A player uses many items to play a baseball game.

Kids and adults of any age can learn to play. It is played in many different parts of the world. Baseball is a very popular sport. Play ball!

Baseball

Baseball is an old game. It started in the 1800s. That is more than 200 years ago! Baseball began in the United States. The game is like two older British games. One game was called cricket. The other game was called rounders. In rounders, the batter was out when someone hit him with the ball! Can you guess why they stopped playing that game?

The game of baseball was fun and new. The game was popular. Kids liked to play. Adults liked to play too.

In 1845, some men made a baseball club. The club was in New York City. One of the men in the club wrote baseball rules. People still use the rules today. The man's name was Alexander Joy Cartwright. He **invented**, or made, the three-strike rule. The three-strike rule means a batter is out if he misses three **pitches,** or throws.

In 1846, the club played a game. The baseball players were in the club. They played against cricket players. Baseball was a fun game for everyone to enjoy, and it still is!

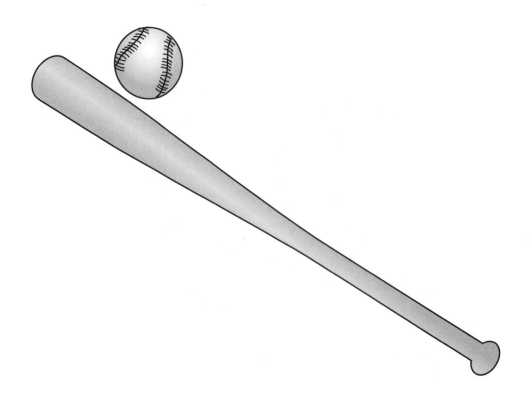

Name _____

Circle the correct answer.

1. Baseball began in

    A. the United States.

    B. Britain.

    C. Canada.

2. A jersey is a type of

    A. bat.

    B. shirt.

    C. glove.

Use the word bank to complete the sentences.

cleats	invented	pitches

3. The baseball player wore spiked _____.

4. The batter missed three _____ and struck out.

5. Alexander Joy Cartwright _____ the three-strike rule.

6. Write a sentence about a baseball game you have seen or played.

_____

_____

_____

Name _____

7. Based on what you read in both passages, draw a picture to show yourself as a baseball player. Label your picture with words from the two passages.

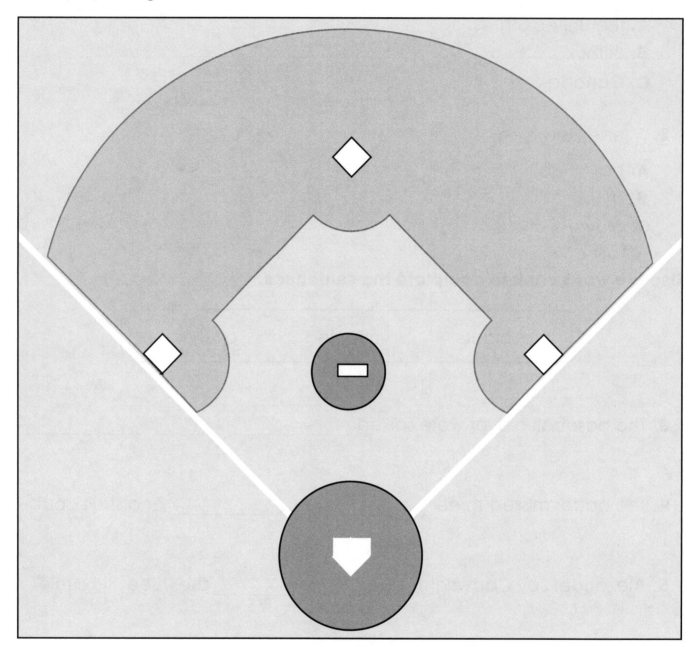

8. How are the two passages different? How are they alike?

_____

_____

_____

TV or a Book?

A TV is not the same as a book. They are two different things. Watching a TV show is not the same as reading a book. They are two different activities. Which do you like more?

Reading a book can help kids learn new **vocabulary**, or words, to use. Reading is a big part of schoolwork. Many kids read every day. Others read only at school. Reading is a skill that people use throughout their lives.

Even though watching a TV show is not the same as reading a book, kids can still learn things from TV. A teacher can use TV as a tool in the classroom. A teacher can use it to show a movie. The movie can be about something the students are learning in school. A teacher can use TV to show a **video**, or recorded images, from a class field trip.

TVs and books can both be used for learning. Books are older, and TVs are newer. But, both are helpful!

TV History

Television, or TV, lets people watch many kinds of pictures. The pictures are on a screen. The pictures move. People watch shows and movies. Sound comes out of the TV. You can hear music. You can hear people talking.

The first TV sold in the 1920s. That was a very long time ago! The TV had black-and-white pictures. Then, color pictures were made. That was a long time ago too. At first, you could only push buttons on the TV. Then, someone made something called a **remote control**. The remote control had buttons to push. The buttons changed the TV picture. People did not have to walk to the TV to change the picture.

Now, TV screens are thin. They were thick when TVs were first made. TV sets come in many sizes. They can be large or small. They come in different shapes. There are some TVs that are curved. They come in a lot of colors! They even come in red! TVs can be found in places all around the world.

Name _____

Circle the correct answer.

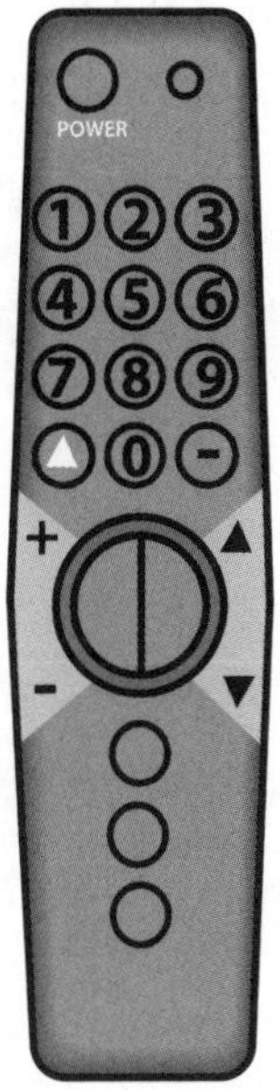

1. The first TVs had a

   A. color picture.

   B. black-and-white picture.

   C. remote control.

2. _____ is a skill used for life.

   A. Reading

   B. Watching TV

   C. Watching videos

Use the word bank to complete the sentences.

> remote control   video   vocabulary

3. As you learn new words, your _____ grows.

4. We watched a _____ about whales.

5. Dad used the _____ to change the channel.

6. Would you rather read a book or watch a TV show? Why?

   _____

   _____

   _____

7. Look back at both passages. Complete the chart with information from the two passages.

TV or a Book?	TV History
Main Idea	Main Idea
New Things I Learned	New Things I Learned

8. How are the two passages alike?

_____

_____

_____

Kim and Rex

Kim has a small dog. She found him at an **animal shelter**. Her father told her that an animal shelter is where animals live when they do not have homes.

"The animal shelter saves animals from bad homes. It also saves some animals from living in the streets. Sometimes, people have to give up their pets when they move," her father explained.

Kim loves her small dog. His name is Rex. Rex is brown and white. He has a black nose. He has pointy ears. Kim is not sure what kind of dog he is. But, Rex is very fast. Rex likes to run!

Rex runs outside every day. Kim throws a ball. Rex gets the ball and brings it back to Kim. Kim also throws a flying disk. Rex jumps up! He catches it in the air. Sometimes, Rex even does a flip!

The Animal Shelter

Lucy lives next to an animal shelter. It is a house for animals that need homes. The shelter workers take care of the animals. Many kinds of dogs and cats live at the shelter. Some animal shelters have birds and small animals. Other animal shelters even have reptiles! Lucy likes to visit the animals.

People take animals that need to be **rescued**, or saved, to the animal shelter. The animals live there for a while. Shelter workers feed them every day and give them fresh water. The animals can have nice beds to rest in. Sometimes, Lucy sees the workers taking the animals outside for walks.

The animals get the care they need. They grow strong. They feel happy. People pet them and love them! Soon, people will come to **adopt**, or take home, the animals. They will go to happy, loving homes.

Lucy looks at the dogs and cats. They are friendly. They want her to talk to them. The workers let her pet them. Maybe Lucy can take one of the animals home with her. She will ask her mother today!

Name _____

Circle the correct answer.

I. Animal shelters have animals such as

A. fish.

B. cats and dogs.

C. butterflies.

2. What does Rex do when Kim throws the ball?

A. runs around in circles

B. gets it and brings it back to Kim

C. catches it in the air

Use the word bank to complete the sentences.

adopt   animal shelter   rescued

3. My brother wants to _____ a new kitten.

4. We went to the _____ to get a new puppy.

5. Workers at the animal shelter _____ Fluffy the cat.

6. Would you like to work in an animal shelter? Why or why not?

_____

_____

_____

Name _____

7. Look back at both passages. Draw an animal you might find at an animal shelter in each box. Then, draw one thing a shelter worker might provide for each animal.

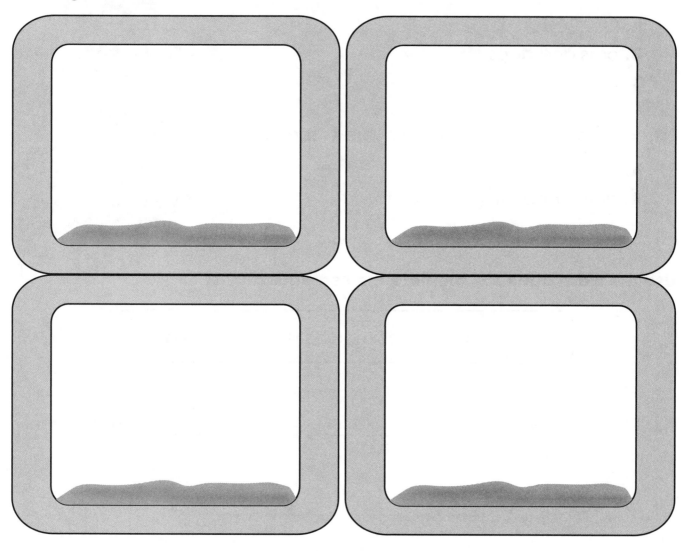

8. How are Kim and Lucy alike?

_____

_____

_____

_____

_____

Play Soccer!

Mel likes to play at recess. He eats his lunch. Then, he goes outside to play with his friends. Most of the time, they slide down the slide one at a time. They also swing on the tire swing. But, today, Mel's friend Ron brought a soccer ball to school. It is his lucky soccer ball. Ron uses it for practice on the weekends.

"Kick the ball over here, Ron!" Mel yelled.

"Sure thing, Mel!" Ron called.

The ball went flying into the air. It was an excellent kick! The ball landed right in front of Mel's feet. Mel kicked the ball with his left foot and then his right foot. He kicked it back and forth, or **dribbled** it, while running. Ron ran quickly across the field. He also kicked the ball. Mel and Ron kicked the ball together.

At the end of recess, Ron picked up his soccer ball. The boys went into their classroom.

"That was so fun!" Ron said.

"Yes, please bring your ball again tomorrow," Mel said.

How to Play Soccer

Luis is learning about soccer. Soccer is more than just kicking a ball. The game of soccer has rules. Luis can kick the ball. He can even bounce the ball on his knees. He can bounce the ball off of his head! But, he cannot touch the ball with his hands at all.

A soccer team has 10 players in the field and one goalie. The goalie **guards**, or watches, the goal. The goal is usually a net. The goalie tries to keep the soccer ball from getting inside the net. Luis wants to be a goalie some day.

The team has a coach. The coach teaches the players how to play better. Luis's coach is named Mr. Gonzalez. A soccer game also has a referee. A **referee** makes sure that the game is being played correctly.

Luis must get the ball into the goal. When the ball goes into the net, Luis's team gets a point. The team with the most goals wins the game.

Name _____

Circle the correct answer.

1. The boys play soccer at

    A. Mel's house.

    B. school.

    C. Ron's house.

2. How many soccer players are on a soccer team?

    A. 11

    B. 9

    C. 10

Use the word bank to complete the sentences.

> dribbled   guards   referee

3. We _____ the ball back and forth.

4. The _____ made sure that the players were following the rules.

5. The goalie _____ the net so that the other team cannot score.

6. Write a sentence about a soccer game you have played or seen.

_____

_____

Name _____

7. Write a letter to tell a friend what you know about the game of soccer. Include facts from the two passages in your letter.

Today's date: _____

Dear _____,

_____

_____

_____

_____

_____

_____

_____

Your friend,

_____

8. How are Mel, Ron, and Luis alike?

_____

_____

_____

_____

Camping with Dad

"Are you done packing, Billy?" Dad asked. Today, Dad and Billy are going on a camping trip. They will drive to the campsite in Dad's truck. Dad and Billy are both excited about the trip.

"I am almost done, Dad! I just need to find my flashlight," Billy said. He looked everywhere for his flashlight but could not find it. He looked in the closet. He looked under the bed. He even looked behind the fish tank. Then, he found it!

"Here I come, Dad!" Billy yelled from his room. Dad was packing the back of the truck. He put in the tent. He put in the grill. He put in the sleeping bags. He put in some fishing poles.

They got into the truck and went to the campsite. The **campsite** is where they will camp. They will put up their tent there. They will sleep there.

Dad asked Billy to get some rocks and sticks. Billy found a lot of rocks and sticks in the woods and down by the river. Dad built a fire. They roasted marshmallows together!

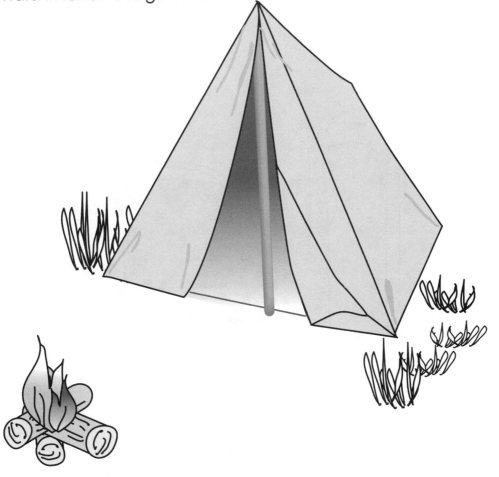

What Do I Pack?

Wanda likes to go camping. It is important that she is **prepared**. When people are prepared, they have all of the right things with them. People need to have gear when camping. Gear is just what Wanda needs.

When Wanda gets ready to go camping, she needs a list. She has to make sure that she has the right clothes for the weather. If it will be hot, she will need light clothes. If it will be cold, she will need heavy clothes. She will need blankets. She can also take a sleeping bag. Some people sleep on air mattresses. Wanda wants to bring a soft pillow.

Wanda has to have food. Some people cook food when they camp. They cook it over a grill or a small pan over a fire. Some people eat food that does not need to be kept cold or warmed up. Wanda thinks apples and bananas are great to take along. She will bring marshmallows. She will roast them on a stick!

Clean water is also a **necessity**, or something that Wanda needs. She will take bottles of fresh water. She will also want to take games to play or books to read.

Circle the correct answer.

1. Wanda will bring marshmallows to

    A. put on her apple.

    B. put in her hot chocolate.

    C. roast on a stick.

2. Billy could not find his

    A. bag.

    B. flashlight.

    C. water.

Use the word bank to complete the sentences.

> campsite   necessity   prepared

3. Wanda is _____ to go camping.

4. The _____ is near the river.

5. Water is a _____ when camping overnight.

6. Would you like to go camping? Why or why not?

_____

_____

_____

7. Imagine that you are getting ready to go camping. You need a list of things to bring so that you are prepared. Use the two passages to make your list.

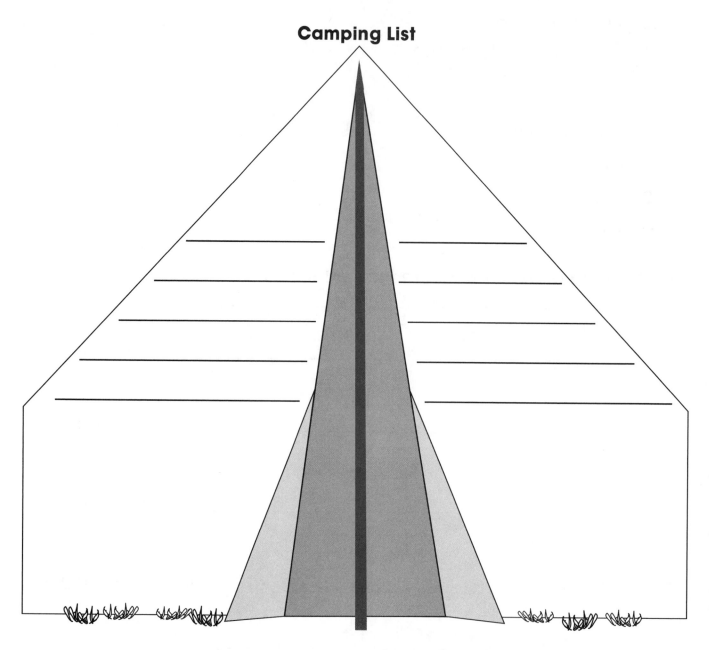

Camping List

8. What new ideas did you learn about camping from the two passages?

_____

_____

_____

Cleaning with Grandma

Grandma comes over to Kelsey's house each week. She helps Kelsey's mom. Kelsey lives with her five brothers and sisters. The house can get messy! So, Grandma comes over to lend a helping hand.

Grandma gives each kid a room to clean. Kelsey always gets the playroom. The playroom has toys that need to be put away. The toys need to go in the **toy chest**, or toy box. The playroom has many books. The books have to go back on the shelves. Sometimes, Kelsey finds old snacks. She has to pick up the crumbs. She also uses the vacuum cleaner.

Kelsey cleans the windows. She sprays the windows. She wipes them dry with a paper towel. Then, Kelsey wipes the table. She puts the crafts away. She puts the glue away. She puts all of the markers into the box.

Grandma comes to see how Kelsey is doing. She is happy to see that the room is clean!

"You did a good job, Kelsey!" Grandma says happily.

Natural Cleaning

Mom cleans the living room. Cory helps her. Cory and Mom use some things you may have in your house that are good for cleaning. These things can be put in a spray bottle. They are not chemicals.

Lemons have acid. This acid makes lemon juice good for cleaning. It is good for cleaning floors and tables. Some people add lemon juice to the dishes in the sink. It helps clean the grease from pots and pans.

Baking soda can make **odors**, or smells, go away. Mom keeps baking soda in the refrigerator. Baking soda is also good for cleaning stains off of coffee mugs. It can get tea stains off of teacups. Baking soda can even **remove**, or take off, crayon marks from walls.

Vinegar is helpful too. It is good for cleaning drains and pipes. It is good for cleaning sinks. Some people add vinegar to the dishes in the sink or the dishwasher. People even use vinegar to clean windows!

Cory and Mom use lemons. They use baking soda and vinegar. They love to clean together!

Circle the correct answer.

1. Kelsey always gets to clean the

    A. playroom.

    B. kitchen.

    C. dining room.

2. What do Cory and her mom use to clean with?

    A. chemicals

    B. lemons, baking soda, and vinegar

    C. tea

Use the word bank to complete the sentences.

odors	remove	toy chest

3. Baking soda can _____ crayon marks from walls.

4. Baking soda can take away _____.

5. Kelsey put the toys back into the _____.

6. Write a sentence about cleaning your room.

_____

_____

_____

Name _____

7. Look back at the two passages. Make a list of things that people can use to clean with. Complete the chart.

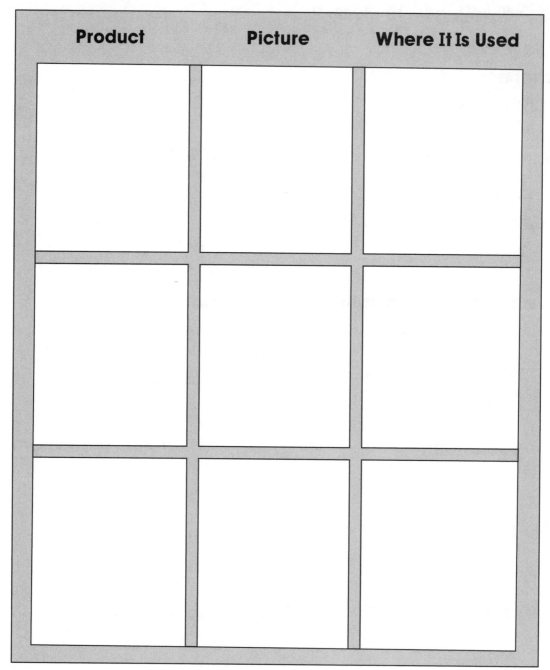

Product	Picture	Where It Is Used

8. Think about the two passages. What new ideas did you read about that will help you clean your room?

_____

_____

_____

Beach Day

Lin goes to the beach every summer with her neighbor Katie. Lin and Katie are great friends. They have lived next door to each other since they were babies. They like going to the beach with their parents when school is over in June.

At the beach, Lin and Katie play in the sand. They use their shovels to dig. They use their buckets to get water. They mix the sand with the water to build a sand castle. They fill the sand molds with water and sand. The wet sand takes the shape of the bucket. Lin and Katie flip over the bucket, and out comes the sand castle!

Lin and Katie play in the ocean. They swim, but they stay close to the beach. The lifeguard watches them from a chair. The lifeguard makes sure that Lin and Katie are safe. Their parents watch them too.

When Lin and Katie get back on the beach, they look for shells. They bring the shells back to the sand castle. They **decorate** the sand castle with the shells to make it look nicer.

Beach Sand

Kendall walked along the beach with her brother, Shawn. They liked to feel the sand in their toes. They walked to the water.

"Shawn, do you know why each piece of sand on the beach is so small?" Kendall asked.

Shawn did not know. He shook his head.

Kendall said, "It is because the sand is broken rocks. The rocks have been worn down over many years. The rocks crumble, or break into small pieces, and turn into sand."

"Yes, I forgot. My class learned that at school this week. The size and color of the sand gives information about the beach. The sand tells what rocks are found in the water and in the beach," Shawn said.

"Yes! We did too. We learned that every beach is a **habitat**, or place where animals and people live. A habitat has plants too," she said.

Kendall and Shawn know that the beach is full of life. They like to walk along the beach. They find many treasures there.

Circle the correct answer.

1. Lin and Katie are

    A. babies.

    B. sisters.

    C. neighbors.

2. Who is Shawn's sister?

    A. Kendall

    B. Lin

    C. Katie

Use the word bank to complete the sentences.

> crumble   decorate   habitat

3. The crabs live in a beach _____.

4. The rocks _____, and over time, they become sand.

5. The girls will _____ the sand castle with shells.

6. Write a sentence about the beach.

_____

_____

7. Look back at both passages. Write six facts you learned about the beach in the graphic organizer.

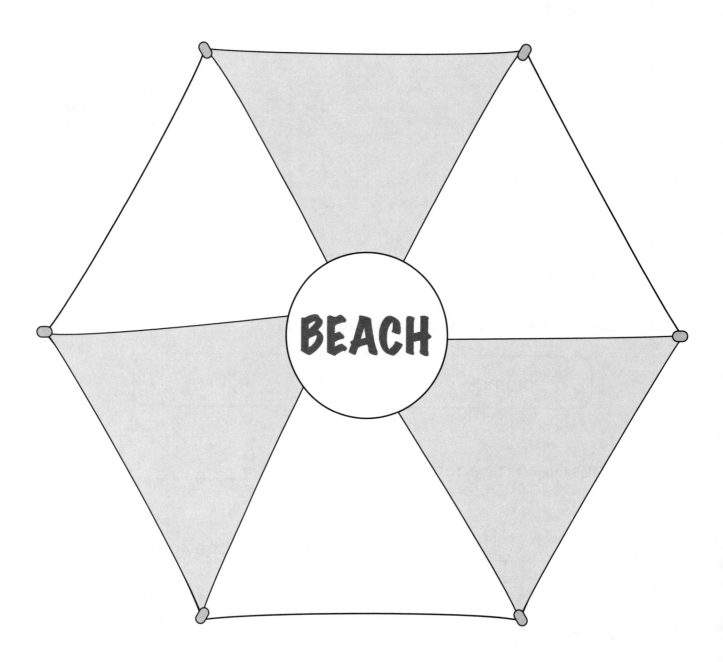

8. Would you like to go to the beach with Lucy and Katie, or with Kendall and Shawn? Explain your answer.

_____

_____

_____

Hiking in the Woods

The camp kids were going on a hike in the woods. They had water bottles and snacks in their backpacks. They were walking with their camp counselor, Ginny. Ginny led the kids into the woods. They all stayed on the path. They followed Ginny.

Ginny showed the kids **poisonous**, or dangerous, plants to stay away from. One of them was poison ivy. She showed the kids what it looked like. The kids knew to stay away from it. They did not want to get a rash. The rash would itch!

Ginny made sure that the kids drank their water. It is important to stay **hydrated**, or filled with water. They also ate their snacks to give them new energy. They climbed up rocks and over fallen trees. They climbed over sticks and branches.

They made it to the top of a hill. The kids sat on a large rock. They looked at the view. They could see their campsite below. The sun was high in the sky. It was hot but so nice to be in the fresh air!

Hiking

Hiking is a great hobby. Laura likes to hike with her aunt. She likes to help plan the hikes. She can choose a hike that is close to or far from her home. She can plan hikes in the woods, on a mountain, or even in a city. Hikes can be over long or short distances. The **distance** is the length of the hike.

Laura finds interesting things on hikes. She sees cool rocks. She sees weird bugs. Sometimes, she sees pretty butterflies. She has often seen a fresh stump or a fallen tree. Animals are always around during a hike. Laura can listen to birdcalls. She would like to be able to know which birds are making each sound.

Laura makes sure to pack plenty of snacks for a hike. Granola is very good. Peanut butter gives kids energy. Also, crackers and fruits can be very tasty. It is important to take along fresh water too. Laura will have a great hike!

Name _____

Circle the correct answer.

1. Where are the camp kids hiking?

   A. at the beach

   B. in the woods

   C. in the city

2. On a hike, people can see

   A. bugs and insects.

   B. TVs.

   C. computers.

Use the word bank to complete the sentences.

> distance   hydrated   poisonous

3. The _____ to the lake was 1 mile (1.6 km).

4. The kids drank water to stay _____.

5. _____ plants can cause an itchy rash.

6. Write a sentence about hiking.

_____

_____

_____

Name _____

7. Imagine that you are going on a hike with your class. Look back at both passages. Make a list of do's and don'ts.

DO'S

DON'TS

8. Based on the two passages, what are the most important things to take along on a hike? Explain why they are important.

Jason's Garden

Jason lives in a small apartment. He has a porch. His mom lets him keep some plants on the porch. He has a few big planters filled with fresh **soil**, or dirt. The soil is full of plant **nutrients**, or minerals. The soil keeps his plants healthy. Jason waters the plants. The plants also get a lot of sun on the porch.

During the spring and summer, Jason grows vegetables. He likes to grow beans and cucumbers. Jason likes to grow these vegetables because his favorite color is green. He also likes to grow tomatoes. He grows two kinds. One kind is big, and one is small. Jason puts the big tomatoes in sandwiches. The small tomatoes are called grape tomatoes. They are the size of grapes. They taste sweet!

Jason grows mint too. It has its own planter because it is so wild. It grows very fast and very large. Jason has to cut it every day in the summertime. His mom likes to put mint leaves in her lemonade. Sometimes, they make iced tea with mint. It is yummy!

Fiction

Family Tree

Growing a garden is so much fun for Dwayne! He can watch the plants grow and get big. He does not always have to plant fruits and vegetables. He does not always have to plant herbs and flowers. Do you know what else he can plant? A tree!

A family may plant a tree together. They call it their family tree. The people in the family get together and plant it in a special spot. They dig a hole with a shovel. They put the **sapling**, or baby tree, into the ground. They cover the hole with soil. They water the tree. It gets sun and grows strong. The family can watch it grow.

Dwayne's family will plant a tree. They will put stones or rocks around the tree. They will put wood chips around it to keep the soil wet. Wet soil helps to keep the tree roots healthy. They know that the tree will be there for a long time, just like their family.

Name _____

Circle the correct answer.

1. What do healthy tree roots need?

   A. rocks

   B. wet soil

   C. stones

2. Jason's mom likes to put mint in her

   A. milk.

   B. water.

   C. lemonade.

Use the word bank to complete the sentences.

nutrients	sapling	soil

3. You can put wood chips around a tree to keep the

   _____ wet.

4. A baby tree is called a _____.

5. Plants need _____ in the soil to keep them healthy.

6. Write a sentence about your favorite plant.

   _____

   _____

Name _____

7. Jason and Dwayne enjoy growing plants and trees. Complete the Venn diagram with facts that describe the way they garden.

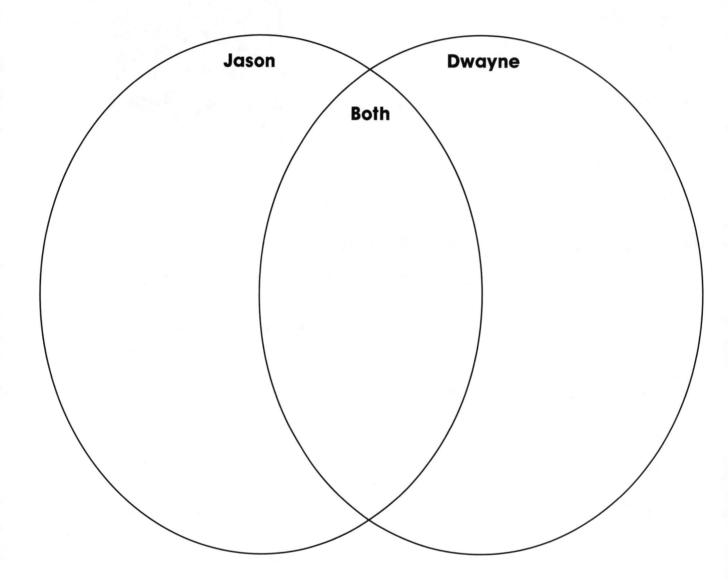

Jason   Dwayne

Both

8. How are the two passages different?

_____

_____

_____

Answer Key

Page 7–8
1. C; 2. A; 3. bill;
4. acorns; 5. fruit;
6. Answers will vary but may include that Joe and Lu like to splash in the birdbath.
7. Woodpecker: eats insects; Drawings will vary. Heron: eats fish, Drawings will vary. Hummingbird: drinks nectar; Drawings will vary. Blue Jay: eats acorns and seeds; Drawings will vary.
8. Answers will vary but may include that both passages are about birds.

Page 11–12
1. A; 2. B; 3. huge;
4. sunflower; 5. kapok;
6. Answers will vary but may include that the sunflower is not as tall as a kapok tree.
7. Sunflower: green and yellow, six feet tall, garden; Kapok tree: green, white, and pink; 200 feet (61 m) tall; Amazon rain forest; Drawings will vary.
8. Answers will vary but may include that they are different heights.

Page 15–16
1. B; 2. C; 3. bait; 4. cast;
5. license; 6. Answers will vary. 7. Answers will vary but should include information from both passages. 8. Answers will vary but may include that the first passage was written to entertain and the second passage was written to inform.

Page 19–20
1. A; 2. C; 3. practice;
4. house; 5. performed;
6. Answers will vary but should be based on personal experiences.
7. Answers will vary but may include that music can make the brain stronger, people can perform music to entertain family and friends, and children can learn to play different musical instruments. 8. Answers will vary.

Page 23–24
1. C; 2. A; 3. bag;
4. ticket; 5. instructions;
6. Answers will vary but may include that the ticket shows the place, time, and date of flight. 7. Answers will

vary but should include four different emotions, drawn and labeled.
8. Answers will vary but should include feelings about flying.

Page 27–28
1. C; 2. B; 3. trim;
4. barber; 5. dye;
6. Answers will vary but may include that a barber or hairdresser cuts hair.
7. Drawings will vary but may include a cloth, scissors, shampoo, spray, gel, brushes, or a hair dryer. 8. Answers will vary but may include that the barber put a cloth around Miguel's neck and cut his hair with scissors.
9. Answers will vary but may include that both passages were about cutting hair.

Page 31–32
1. B; 2. B; 3. guests;
4. gift wrap; 5. invitation;
6. Answers will vary but may include that it has the time and date of the party or that it shows where the party will be.
7. Answers will vary but should include details from both passages.

Answer Key

8. Answers will vary but may include information about a party the student has attended.

Page 35–36
1. A; 2. C; 3. route;
4. repair; 5. detour;
6. Answers will vary.
7. Answers will vary but should include details from the passages.
8. Answers will vary but may include that various trucks and other machines are used in construction by men and women construction workers.

Page 39–40
1. B; 2. B; 3. collect;
4. crumb;
5. communicate;
6. Answers will vary.
7. Drawings should include fruit, crumbs, seeds, and bugs.
8. Answers will vary but may include that both passages give facts about ants.

Page 43–44
1. B; 2. A; 3. license;
4. rent; 5. movers;
6. Answers will vary.
7. Answers will vary but may include books,

toys, clothes, boxes, chairs, and tables.
8. Answers will vary but may include that moving day is a busy day.

Page 47–48
1. A; 2. B; 3. nocturnal;
4. dens; 5. searching;
6. Answers will vary.
7. Answers will vary but should include facts from the passage.
8. Answers will vary but may include that the two passages are alike because they both are about nocturnal animals. They are different because the second passage gives more facts about raccoons.

Page 51–52
1. C; 2. A; 3. art lab;
4. famous; 5. medium;
6. Answers will vary but may include artwork, paintings, sculptures, or dinosaurs. 7. Answers will vary but should include information from both passages. 8. Answers will vary but may include that the first passage tells about different types of museums and the

second passage tells about one museum and what you can do there.

Page 55–56
1. B; 2. B; 3. Thickets;
4. burrow; 5. rustles;
6. Answers will vary.
7. Answers will vary but should include facts from both passages.
8. Answers will vary but may include that one passage is about a rabbit that lives beneath a porch. The other passage gives facts about one type of rabbit.

Page 59–60
1. A; 2. B; 3. cleats;
4. pitches; 5. invented;
6. Answers will vary.
7. Drawings will vary but should include vocabulary words from the passages.
8. Answers will vary but may include that one passage tells about baseball equipment and the other tells about the origins of the game of baseball. Both passages are about baseball.

Page 63–64
1. B; 2. A; 3. vocabulary;

Answer Key

4. video; 5. remote control; 6. Answers will vary.
7. Answers will vary but should include the main idea from each passage and at least two new things learned.
8. Answers will vary but may include that the two passages are alike because they both offer facts about TV.

Page 67–68
1. B; 2. B; 3. adopt;
4. animal shelter;
5. rescued; 6. Answers will vary. 7. Answers will vary but should include information from both passages. 8. Answers will vary but may include that they both care for animals.

Page 71–72
1. B; 2. A; 3. dribbled;
4. referee; 5. guards;
6. Answers will vary.
7. Answers will vary but should include facts about soccer.
8. Answers will vary but may include that they are alike

because they all enjoy playing soccer.

Page 75–76
1. C; 2. B; 3. prepared;
4. campsite;
5. necessity; 6. Answers will vary. 7. Answers will vary but should include details from both passages. 8. Answers will vary but may include that camping requires a lot of gear.

Page 79–80
1. A; 2. B; 3. remove;
4. odors; 5. toy chest;
6. Answers will vary but should include personal details. 7. Answers will vary but should show products read about in the two passages.
8. Answers will vary but should include information from the two passages.

Page 83–84
1. C; 2. A; 3. habitat;
4. crumble; 5. decorate;
6. Answers will vary.
7. Answers will vary but must include facts from the passages.
8. Answers will vary but

should include a choice and reasons.

Page 87–88
1. B; 2. A; 3. distance;
4. hydrated;
5. Poisonous; 6. Answers will vary. 7. Answers will vary but should use details from both passages. 8. Answers will vary but may include water and snacks, for hydration and energy.

Page 91–92
1. B; 2. C; 3. soil;
4. sapling; 5. nutrients;
6. Answers will vary.
7. Answers will vary but could include: (Jason) has a porch garden, grows vegetables, grows mint; (Both) like to garden, can grow different things; (Dwayne) plants a family tree, puts stones and wood chips around it, the tree grows for a long time; 8. Answers will vary but may include that the two passages are about planting different items.

Notes